Read for the Brand

A Tale of the Horse Tooth Fairy

© 2022 by Mary Fichtner
All rights reserved

No part of this book may be reproduced in any form or by any means, electronic or mechanical including photocopy, information storage or a retrieval system without the express and written consent of the author. Reproductions of the cover or brief quotations from the text are permitted when used in conjunction with book reviews by qualified editors or authors.

Illustrations by Roslan Fichtner

Layout and Design by Andy Grachuk
www.JingotheCat.com

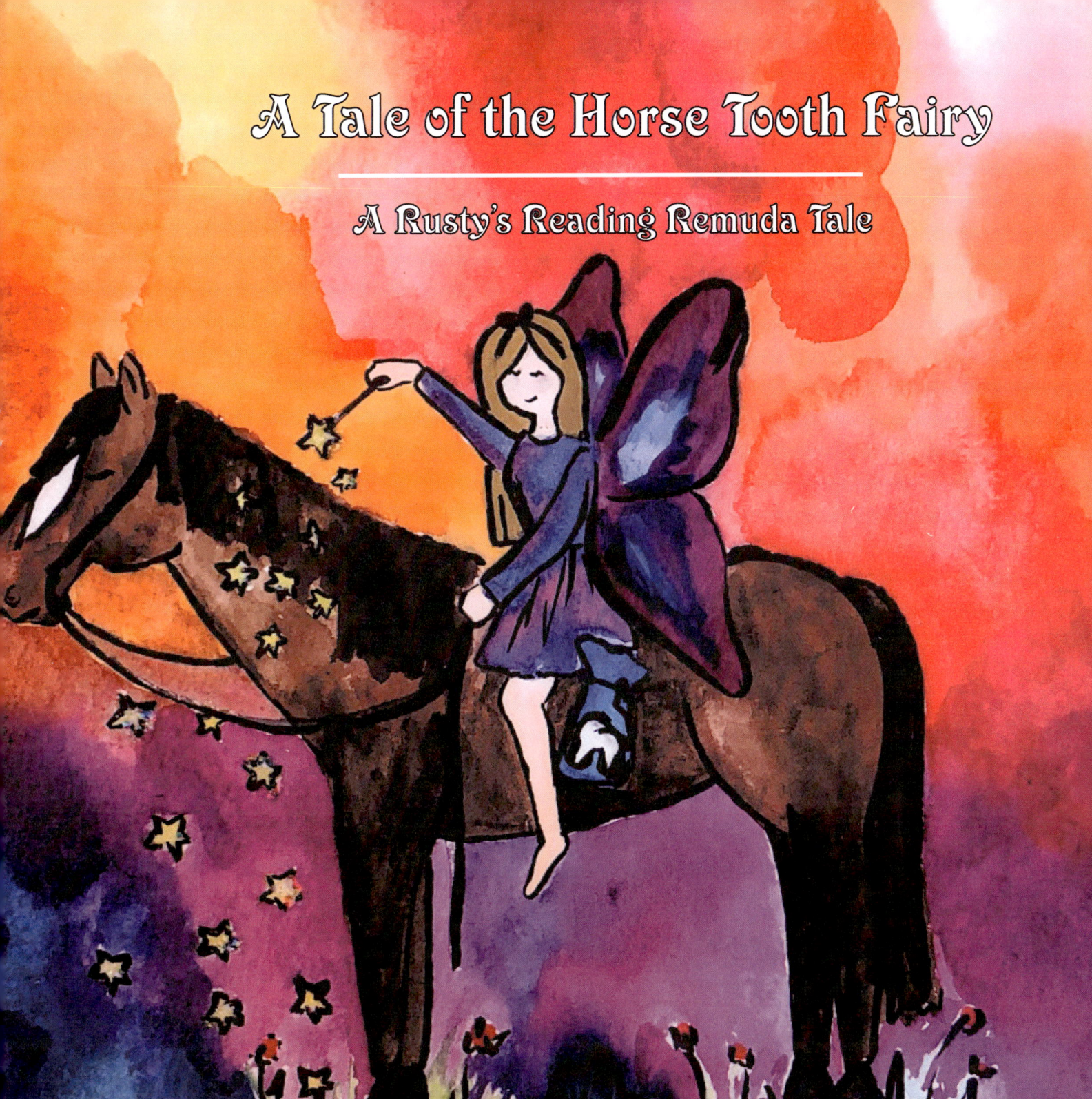

Remarkable is the tooth fairy's skill
From horse to horse she spreads her goodwill
At first, some might grit their teeth just a whit
'til she mixes her sparkles in with their spit

As each special pony learns how to trust
They open up wide to get their teeth brushed
She brings back their smile: they eat better too
Fixing their teeth is what she's called to do

All over she travels, from hither to yon

From the east to the west; even beyond!

To meager stables, she travels forthwith

She won't hesitate, she's a gifted "Tooth-smith"

Sometimes a 'Thank You" is payment enough

As she gives them the gift of a shine and a buff

She performs her tooth magic with a beautiful smile

Enduring and steadfast all of the while

Then off to the castles where ritzy pens stand

A completely opposite, far away land

Expensive and fancy, the barns are so plush

All teeth will be balanced; there will be no rush

These horses are athletes so they must be fit

As she readies their mouths to hold their best bit

Sending them off to perform at their best

Nothing will stop the Tooth Fairy's great quest

Next, her wings fly to beauty indeed

Off to the islands; more horses in need

These equine work hard on polo fields green

A place more stunning than most eyes have seen

These strong horses' mouths hold power galore

As she checks their incisors, molars, and more

The importance their teeth hold can't be overstated

The Tooth Fairy's grit won't be too highly rated

She works on dentition right next to the waves

Floating teeth by the ocean, as horse mouths she saves

Out to the west, under big skies so blue
Where rodeo horses have much work to do
Ranch horses, ropers, barrel horses too
She must go to them, but that's nothing new
It's serious business, the mission of these

The care they must have she provides with a breeze
If their bit seats don't get the very best care
They cannot perform their great feats with flare
As she works hard the sparkles fly from her wand
Creating a wonderful, powerful bond

Then off to Australia, the Land Down Under

To help colts and fillies whose teeth shed asunder

The Tooth Fairy blesses these precious young ones

Around two years old; taught how to run

Each race is important and speed is a must

Their baby teeth (caps) need much fairy dust

So they can perform their best race with ease

The Melbourne Cup, The Big Win to seize

Who knows where the Tooth Fairy might show up next?

All she accomplishes leave some perplexed

Across the big globe, no place is too far

She uses her wings, no need for a car

Gritty and eager, her mission so true

Balancing horse mouths; making them new

Older or young, no matter their age

She makes them all smile, gives them happy days

So, here's to hoping she visits you too

With her mystical fairy dust, so tried and true

Just like the denim we love, old or new!

Mary - Author • Roslan - Illustrator

Mary and Roslan believe we all have gifts that lead us to our purpose. After meeting Ashley, we learned we all share that belief and loved how she is living her passion and purpose. This led us to the decision to merge our gifts and create a fun story highlighting our Purpose Power! We believe in your purpose too! Here's to your journey and hoping we see you on down the trail.

Aloha & Howdy, I'm Ashley! I'm a Doer, a Dentist, and a purveyor of all things Denim. Hence the name of my equine dental business, 'Denim Dentistry'. I'm a real-life tooth fairy, but for horses! I call the small rural community of Unionville, Missouri home when I'm not traveling to and from clients. I come from a long lineage of agriculturalists and consider myself an advocate of the western lifestyle. I graduated college with not one, but two degrees. I attained a Bachelor's of Science in Biology from Missouri Southern State University and a Bachelor's in Bi-Vocational Ministry from Ozark Christian College. I have a Master's of Science in Agriculture degree from Sam Houston State University. I am continuously working towards advancing the industry of equine dentistry with scientific studies and published findings. In my free time, I like to read, write, and run. I pray this book inspires you to cultivate a passion and to proceed without boundaries to serve those in need. God bless.

Read for the Brand

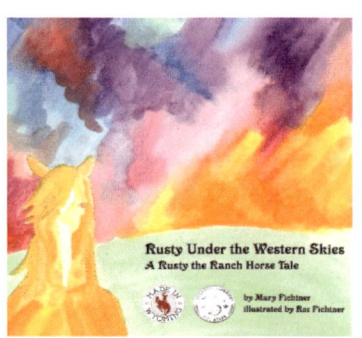
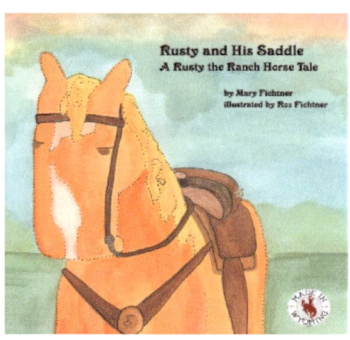

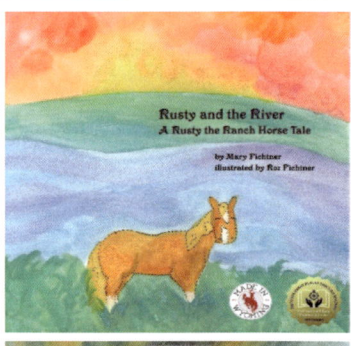
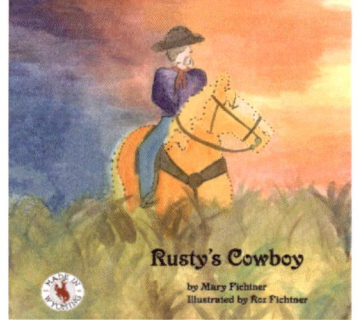
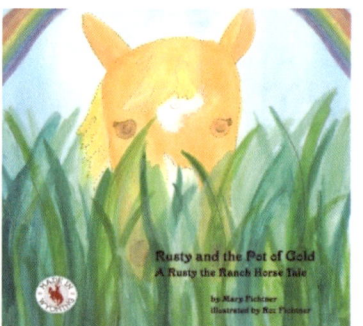
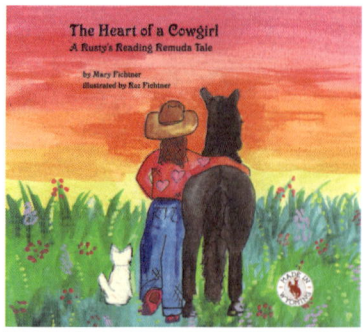
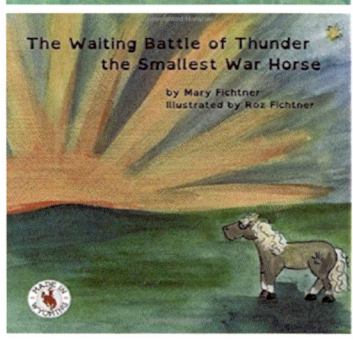

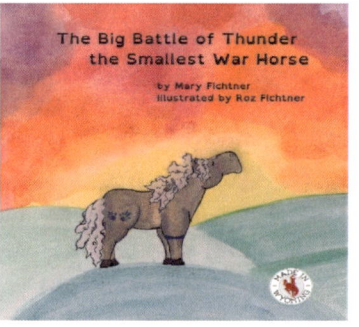

www.ingramcontent.com/pod-product-compliance
Lightning Source LLC
Chambersburg PA
CBRC091453160426
43209CB00024B/1885